chimp

Jinny Johnson

MARSHALL PUBLISHING • LONDON

When chimps are very small, their mothers carry them everywhere. Bala stood up for the first time when he was six months old.

Bala runs around on four legs. But he can also stand up on two legs, just like you. He is good at climbing trees, too.

Baby chimps drink
their mother's milk.
Now Bala is bigger,
he also eats leaves,
insects and fruit.

Bala has seen his mother use a stick to get tasty termites out of their nest. He tries to copy her, but he is not very good at it yet!

Young chimps like to explore and play. They love being tickled! But if he feels scared, Bala runs back to his mother for a hug.

Chimps sleep in nests that they have made up in the trees.